This library edition published in 2011 by Walter Foster Publishing, Inc.
Walter Foster Library
Distributed by Black Rabbit Books
P.O. Box 3263 Mankato, Minnesota 56002

Printed in China, Shanghai Offset Printing Products Limited, Shenzhen.

First Library Edition

Library of Congress Cataloging-in-Publication Data

Cardaci, Diane.
  Flowers & botanicals / by Diane Cardaci. -- 1st library ed.
     p. cm. -- (Drawing made easy)
  ISBN 978-1-936309-10-8
  1. Flowers in art. 2. Plants in art. 3. Drawing--Technique. 4. Botanical illustration.
I. Title. II. Title: Flowers and botanicals.
  NC815.C37 2011
  743'.73--dc22

                                                                    2010005321

022010
0P1815

9 8 7 6 5 4 3 2 1

DRAWING
MADE
EASY

FLOWERS &
BOTANICALS

By Diane Cardaci

Walter Foster

www.walterfoster.com

CONTENTS

INTRODUCTION

Flowers hold a universal appeal for people all over the world. We use them to speak for us, giving flowers to express emotion, love, friendship, and sympathy. We are fascinated by their colors, but underneath the enchanting rainbow of hues is an incredible beauty of form, structure, and value. That beauty can be captured by the simplest of tools: the drawing pencil.

With the delicate touch of a pencil, we can capture the gentle fold of a bell flower or the intricate detail of an opening bud. We can develop the deep shadows of a twisted leaf or the dark center of a sunflower to make our drawings come to life.

It is with great pleasure that I invite you to look over my shoulder to see how I meet the challenge of portraying the splendor of the world of flowers and botanicals. The foundation of all drawing is observation. The lessons in this book are designed to help you simplify what you are seeing, first by using basic lines and angles, then progressing to depiction of the organic shapes, and finally adding the tonal shading to develop the forms. Throughout these pages, I share skills that I have learned from other artists, as well as some techniques that I have developed through my own experimentation. I encourage you to experiment on your own and approach the exercises with a joyful heart.

TOOLS AND MATERIALS

The first step for any drawing project is to gather the tools and materials you need for drawing. This process requires several decisions as to how you will work and with which materials you are most comfortable. The tools and materials detailed here will help you get started.

Sharpeners I usually use an electric sharpener indoors and a handheld sharpener outdoors. Carpenter's pencils and soft pencils like carbon and charcoal are best sharpened manually with a single-edge blade and a sandpaper block. The shavings can be saved and used as graphite or charcoal powder (see "Graphite Powder" on page 12). Lead holders use special sharpeners called "pointers."

Workspace Work where you feel most comfortable drawing and where you can concentrate; it could be in your kitchen with a drawing board leaning against a table or in a studio with a professional drafting table or easel. To avoid eye strain, be sure you have good, direct lighting, with no shadows on your drawing surface. If you sit to draw, be sure your chair provides good support for your back. It is also good to have a separate, small table or taboret within easy reach to hold your drawing supplies. (I tend to draw standing up because then I can step back to view my work as it progresses.) You also will need a smooth surface to hold your drawing as you work—anything from a portable drawing board to a drawing table or easel that tilts at various angles for comfort. I like a large drawing surface so I can tape my reference photos next to my drawing.

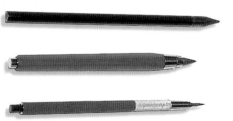

Woodless graphite pencil

Large lead holder

Small lead holder

Other Types of Pencils Water-soluble graphite pencils, also known as "wash pencils," let you create interesting effects by manipulating the pencil strokes with a wet brush. (See page 12.) Carpenter's pencils are wide graphite pencils that create broad strokes. Carbon pencils—which combine some of the best qualities of charcoal and graphite—and charcoal pencils create darker tones without the shine that is characteristic of graphite pencil drawings.

Graphite Pencils High-quality graphite pencils can be found in art and craft stores. They range in grade from hard (H) to soft (B); numbers indicate the degree of hardness or softness, with 9H being the hardest and 9B being the softest. I prefer pencils from the B range and use the 2H for sharp details and outlining. The harder the lead, the sharper and lighter the lines. The graphite lead typically is encased in wood, although there also are woodless pencils (with a lacquer coating) and metal or plastic lead holders, which can accommodate various sizes and grades of lead.

Papers The appearance of your drawing is greatly affected by the paper you choose. Most high-quality drawing papers are available in textured *(vellum-finish)* or smooth *(plate-finish)* surfaces. I like to use a thick, sturdy paper called "Bristol paper" (which is different from the pasteboard called "Bristol board" commercial artists use). When drawing light, delicate petals and soft details, I use smooth-finish Bristol paper so no bumpy texture interferes with the drawing. When I want a bit of built-in texture, I use vellum-finish Bristol paper, as the slight texture allows me to create deeper tones. The texture helps break up the drawing and is great for depicting bark and stones. Always choose acid-free papers so your drawing will not yellow or deteriorate with age.

Sketchbooks Sketchbooks come in a variety of sizes and textures, just like loose drawing paper. Spiral-bound sketchbooks are great when you're drawing on the go. Book-bound sketchbooks keep your sketches better protected for long-term storage. I like to keep a small sketchbook with me at all times in case I see something beautiful and inspiring. This is especially helpful when drawing flowers because we see most flora while outdoors.

Transferring an Image

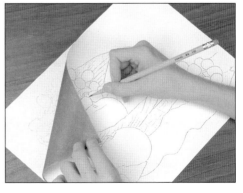

I suggest that you start your drawings on a piece of tracing vellum so you can rework and refine the drawing before transferring it to your final art paper. Tracing vellum is a heavyweight, translucent paper that withstands heavy erasing. (Note that tracing vellum is different from vellum-finish Bristol paper.) When you're satisfied with your initial drawing, turn over the tracing vellum and cover the back with an even coat of graphite. Then place the vellum on top of your art paper, graphite-side down. Trace over the lines you want to keep with a hard 2H pencil. The pressure of your pencil will transfer the lines to the art paper below. (Another method involves transfer paper, which is a sheet of paper coated on one side with graphite. Simply place one sheet—graphite-side down—between the tracing vellum and art paper before you trace.) Occasionally lift the corner of the tracing vellum (and the transfer paper, if applicable) to make sure the lines are transferring correctly. After the lines have been transferred, make any corrections and clean up the drawing with a kneaded eraser.

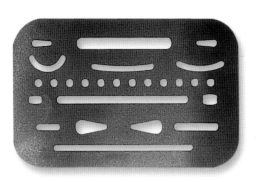

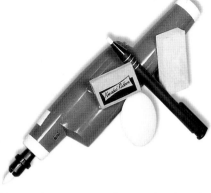

Eraser Shield An eraser shield acts like a stencil and can be used with any eraser to mask off part of the drawing, allowing for precise lines and shapes.

Erasers I use erasers not only to erase but also as drawing tools to "lift out" graphite and create lighter tones (see page 13). Kneaded erasers can be molded into whatever shape you wish and do not leave crumbs. Vinyl erasers are capable of erasing darker lines. For stubborn marks, you may want a battery-powered eraser, but be careful because it can damage the paper.

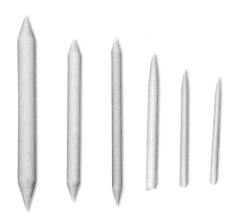

◄ **Blending Tools** Because skin contains oils, you should avoid using your fingers to blend graphite. Instead you can use paper blending stumps and *tortillons,* which look like white paper pencils and come in different diameters. Blending stumps (far left) are pointed on both ends, whereas tortillons (near left) are pointed on one end. Chamois cloths also are commonly used to blend large areas and create interesting effects; roll or fold the cloth to make a point for smaller areas. Felt and tissue paper also can be used for blending.

Additional Tools

You often will need drafting tape to secure your drawing to the board; but never put tape directly on the drawing area of the paper because it will leave a sticky residue. Rulers and triangles come in handy for drawing straight edges, such as those needed for a table or a cube-shaped container. To hold a flower in place for drawing, I like to insert it in florist's foam (pictured under ruler). I also keep a camera handy so I can take photos to reference while drawing.

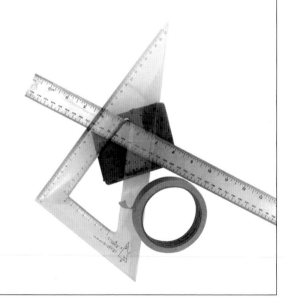

ANATOMY OF THE FLOWER

Although we are artists and not scientists, understanding the basic anatomy of a flower will help us sharpen our observational skills. Use a magnifying glass to study the very small parts of a flower to better understand the shape of the petal, how leaves connect to stems, how buds develop, and so forth. This also will help you to recognize the individuality of each flower. As you train your eye to see more, you gradually will learn to pick out the important details that add realism to your drawing.

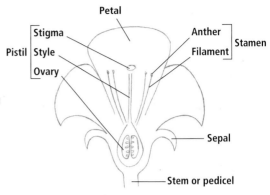

Stem Take care when drawing the point where a leaf joins the stem—this area has details that are different from the rest of the stem. For example, note the joints and the changes in shading around them.

Bud Before a flower blooms, it exists as a small bud. Without a proper highlight, the roundness of the teardrop shape may become lost.

Branch Branches often are thick and rough, with uneven surfaces. Their texture adds personality and variation to your drawings.

Tree Flowers Blossoms on trees are different from those growing out of the ground. The delicate petals on gnarled branches provide a lovely contrast.

BLOCKING IN BASIC SHAPES

Drawing flowers can seem challenging because of their intricate detail, but you will find it much easier if you start with the lines and angles that form the flower's basic shape—a process called "blocking in." Study the flower and look for its basic shape. Is it round or star shaped? Does it look like a cup or a tube? Start with an easy, familiar shape for the outline of the blossom—the most common shapes are the cup, trumpet, bell, star, and modified star. Block in the outside shape of the flower, and then begin to add more basic shapes for the individual petals and leaves. Break down everything into manageable forms, piece by piece. Take your time when blocking in; it is said that the biggest mistakes in a drawing are made in the first five minutes!

Cup Block in the outer shape of the crocus blossom with straight lines, creating a five-sided polygon. Check the proportion of the height to the width. Use straight lines to delineate the spaces between the petals; then go back in and use curved lines to draw the petals.

Trumpet Use long, diverging lines and then a polygon shape to block in the outermost part of the flower. Compare the length of the trumpet with its width and also with the size of the polygon. Draw lines to represent the *negative shapes*—the spaces between and around the actual object; then draw the curves of the flower.

Bell First draw five straight lines to define the shape of the tube of the bell. Then use a triangular shape to determine the opening of the bell, and refine the shape of the opening with three more straight lines. Next draw the curves.

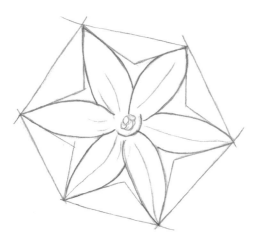 

Star First draw a hexagon, which will encompass the entire blossom. Then draw some V-shaped lines between the points to indicate the negative space between the petals. These lines and angles should be fairly even, as this is a very symmetrical flower. Now you can start drawing the curves that define the petals.

Modified Star Block in this blossom with eight straight lines, again comparing length and width. Add lines to define the negative spaces between the petals, and finally draw the curves of the petals.

CHANGING VIEWPOINTS

The angle at which you view an object determines an object's shape when you are blocking it in. Study how the different views shown below affect the shape of a flower. In each example, I draw the basic shape of the flower below the blossom to better illustrate what is happening to the petunia's shape as the viewpoint changes.

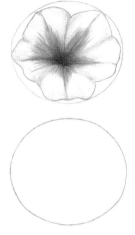  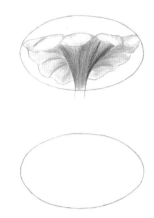

Frontal View In this view, I am looking almost head-on into the petunia. The shape of the petunia fits inside a circle.

Three-Quarter View Now I see the flower from the both the side and front. The circle becomes an ellipse.

Bottom View In this view from the back of the flower, the ellipse becomes even narrower.

Studying Flowers from Different Angles To draw a bouquet like this one, it's important to study flowers from all angles. Flowers in a vase rarely all face the same direction, so learning to accurately depict your flowers at different angles is necessary to achieve a realistic rendering.

SHADING BASICS

Shading gives depth and dimension to your drawings because it creates contrasts in *value,* the relative lightness or darkness of the graphite. To develop a truly three-dimensional representation of a flower, it is imperative to understand how light creates tonal variations on basic shapes. In pencil drawing, values range from black (the darkest value) through different shades of gray to white (the lightest value).

Working with Value Scales

Value scales are tools that you can use to see how value increases gradually as you apply more pressure with the same pencil. When you make your own value scales, you can see which tones your pencils are capable of creating. Work from light to dark, adding more and more tone for successively darker values.

Graphite Value Scale Graphite is capable of producing delicate tonal variations. Place more pressure on the pencil to achieve darker tones. Carbon and graphite can be combined, but the carbon pencil must always be used as the first layer because graphite is very slick and the carbon won't adhere to it.

Carbon Pencil Value Scale Carbon and graphite reflect light differently, so they produce different results. Carbon pencils are capable of creating much darker, deeper shades.

Shading To Create Form and Texture

Every shape or form we see is created by the reaction of the object's surface to light. To create a three-dimensional appearance, the subject must be lit in a way that brings out its form. For example, if you light an object from a three-quarter angle, the object will produce shadows. These shadows accentuate the dimensions of the object. Study the following examples to see how each object's form and texture is evident through the use of lighting and varying values.

Smooth Texture For this drawing, I very lightly shade the top of the ribbon to show that it is in direct light. The deepest shadows appear on the folded part of the ribbon, where it is blocked from the light. The smooth, subtle tones suggest the ribbon's satiny surface.

Dense Texture I create the dense texture of this flower by heavily shading the lower left side with short, scribbled strokes. I leave the top right side lighter to show the direction of the light source.

Cup-Shaped Flower To accurately shade this flower, look at the shadows as the petal starts to fold outward. The value is lighter where the flower folds out, whereas the inside of the flower receives less light and remains shadowed.

Bud I create the shadow along the length of the bud using long, curved strokes. Because the surface is curved, the light that hits one side diminishes as it moves across the form horizontally. If this were a flat object, the light would spread much farther, as it does on the petals of the cup-shaped flower.

Understanding Shadows

There are two main types of shadows: cast shadows and form shadows. A *cast shadow* is what people generally think of as a shadow; it's thrown onto a nearby surface by something blocking the light source. Cast shadows usually have sharp, defined edges, but they aren't solid—they get lighter and less defined as they move away from the object that's creating them. *Form shadows* are the shadows on the areas of an object that are not directly facing the light source. These shadows have softer and less defined edges, and they are lighter than cast shadows because they aren't created by a blocked light source.

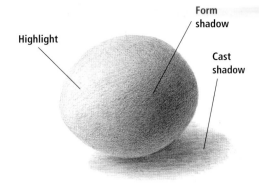

Highlight

Form shadow

Cast shadow

Light and Shadow The highlight is the lightest value, where the light source directly strikes the object. The form shadow is the shadow that is on the object itself. The cast shadow is the shadow that the object casts on the opposite side of the light source.

Revealing Shape Imagine the cylinder above without shading—it would be just a rectangle with a curved top and bottom. But by adding the form shadow on the left and leaving the highlight on the right, the object appears to have a rounded, three-dimensional form.

Identifying Shadows Because the light is coming from above and left, the highlights are on the upper left area of the bud and sepals; the darkest form shadows are on the areas that are directly opposite the light source. The *reflected light,* which bounces back from the surface, also helps give form to the object. The cast shadow is darkest where it is closest to the bud.

Observing Cast Shadows Here a long, thin leaf (not shown) is creating a cast shadow on a flower bud. When the shadow falls across the bud, it wraps around the bud's cylindrical shape (far left). When the same cast shadow falls across this planter, it bends over the planter's angular edge (near left).

SHADING TECHNIQUES

It is a valuable exercise to try drawing a flower using different techniques for creating texture and values. You will find that specific techniques work better for certain flowers. For example, blending works well when there are subtle value changes, but crosshatching (see below) may be better if you want to add more detail to your shading. You also may find that you enjoy using some techniques more than others—this is the beginning of developing your own personal style. Here I've drawn five versions of the same violet, using different shading techniques for each.

Using Different Media

Graphite Powder I dip the tip of a blending stump into some *graphite powder*—dust collected from sharpening soft graphite pencils, such as a 2B. (You also can buy graphite powder in art stores.) I use light pressure and stroke with the stump as if I were shading with the side of a pencil, and I blend in a layer of tone on the shadowed areas of the flower.

Graphite Washes This time I add tone with water-soluble pencils (see page 4). After applying some tone with the water-soluble pencil, I use a damp brush to blend the graphite, creating a thin application— or a *wash*—similar to watercolor paint. It is important to blot your brush on a paper towel to absorb the excess water before applying it to your drawing.

Carbon Pencil Carbon pencils create a very smooth, matte finish. The rich, velvety tones are great for depicting soft textures. For dark areas, I use a soft carbon pencil. For lighter areas, I use a hard carbon pencil with light pressure. The carbon pencil creates deeper darks, but it is harder to achieve very delicate details.

Using Different Strokes

Crosshatching This technique involves making a series of parallel lines (called "hatching"), and then criss-crossing them over one another to create tone (called "crosshatching"). By making the strokes closer together, the shading becomes darker. These strokes are all made with a very sharp point. I lay in some parallel strokes with an HB, following the direction of the petals. Then I go back over the strokes, changing direction and following the curve of the petal.

Stippling I create all the tonal shading in this example using *stippling,* where grouped dots visually merge to create tone when viewed from a distance. The closer the dots, the darker the value. I use a dull 4B pencil and keep adding dots to the drawing, using a greater concentration of them in the darkest areas and only a few dots to depict the lightest areas.

Using Special Techniques

Impressing After sketching the outline of the leaf, I use a small blunt object that doesn't make a mark (such as the chiseled end of a paintbrush) and medium pressure to "draw" the veins, indenting them into the paper. When I shade the leaf with a water-soluble pencil, the impressed veins remain white (instead of being covered by the tone).

Lifting Out First I block in the basic shape of the leaf. Using charcoal powder (shavings from a charcoal pencil) and a blending stump, I shade the leaf. To create the veins, I lift out tone by stroking over the charcoal with a kneaded eraser molded to a point. The white areas represent the veins.

Negative Drawing Here I create the veins by shading only the dark areas *around* the veins (the negative spaces). I use charcoal powder and a stump to smudge the dark areas of the negative space. The stump is too large to be precise, so I go back in using a soft carbon pencil sharpened to a fine point to shade the veins.

SKETCHING BASIC FLOWER PARTS

Just as it's a good idea to practice drawing facial features separately before drawing an entire portrait, it's beneficial to become comfortable drawing individual parts of a flower before creating an entire composition. For example, start out by sketching the head of the flower; then you can progress to the leaves and stems. When you've mastered drawing these basic parts, you can begin to add details. When I sketch, I like to use vellum-finish Bristol paper with a large-diameter, soft-lead pencil, which allows me to loosen up and capture the fluid lines of the flowers and botanicals.

Focusing on Flower Heads

Start your sketches with a simple three-step process. At first you can concentrate on the flower heads only, blocking in the basic shapes, drawing outlines, and then adding details and shading.

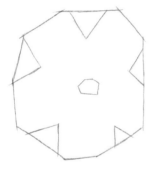  

Step 1 Here I use straight lines to block in the overall shape of the flower. Then I draw five V shapes to delineate the negative space around the petals. I also draw a small circle to block in the pistil and stamens.

Step 2 Now I add the curves of the petals and draw some of the basic lines to indicate the deeper grooves within the petals. These lines help describe the flower's form.

Step 3 I erase the guidelines and then refine the drawing. I add some tone using graphite powder and a narrow stump. Then I use a sharp HB to shade the petals with long, slightly curved strokes.

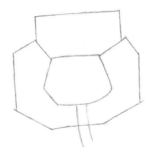  

Step 1 I break down this flower into three basic shapes to block in the general shape, and I also indicate the top of the flower's stem.

Step 2 Next I define the curve at the top of the flower and then add long, needlelike sepals coming out at different angles at the base of the flower.

Step 3 I separate the petals and create their texture with long strokes and a sharp HB. I use a 2B and heavy pressure to shade the lower area. Lastly I shade the sepals with an HB.

Adding Leaves and Stems

Once you're comfortable drawing the head of a flower, you can begin to work on drawing the leaves and stems. There's a lot more to a flower than the petals, so you'll want to pay careful attention to these important elements. Study their different shapes, the vein patterns of the leaves, and the way the leaves attach to the stems.

Basic Leaf First I use some straight lines to establish the basic shape of the leaf. Then I use these lines as a guide to draw the leaf's outline. I draw the main veins of the leaf and then add tone with loose hatch marks.

Twisted Leaf First I use straight lines to block in the shape; then I define the leaf's curves. Using the side of a 6B, I quickly add some tone. The deepest shadows accentuate the folds and bring out the leaf's shape.

Long Leaves I roughly sketch the outlines of these long, slender leaves, then go back and refine their shapes. Using the side of the pencil, I add tone with long, loose strokes to illustrate the thin, lilting leaves.

Thin Stem First I use a sharp point to block in the curving shape of the stem; then I draw the teardrop-shaped leaves. I add a lighter stem sprouting from the main stem. Finally, I add medium tone to the stem and delicate tone to the leaves.

Thorny Stem Here I use several long lines to establish the length, width, and direction of the stem. Then I draw the thorns, paying attention to where and how they connect to the stem. I use long, parallel lines to add tone to the stem.

Stem with Bud Many flowers have small buds growing along the stem. I block in the basic shape of the bud with straight lines and then draw the curves. I use the side of the pencil for lighter tones and heavy pressure for darker tones.

CALLA LILY

The glory of this flower lies in its simplicity and graceful lines. I found this perfect specimen growing on the side of the road, in front of an Italian country home. It had been planted by the man who lives there, placed perfectly so all who pass by can share in his enjoyment of this blooming beauty.

Taking a Closer Look I decide to take a close-up photo of the calla lily blossom so I can focus on its large, graceful shapes and beautiful simplicity.

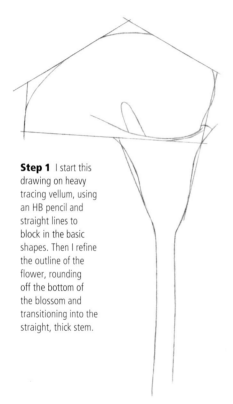

Step 1 I start this drawing on heavy tracing vellum, using an HB pencil and straight lines to block in the basic shapes. Then I refine the outline of the flower, rounding off the bottom of the blossom and transitioning into the straight, thick stem.

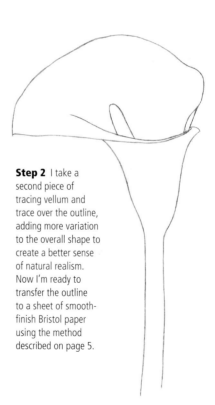

Step 2 I take a second piece of tracing vellum and trace over the outline, adding more variation to the overall shape to create a better sense of natural realism. Now I'm ready to transfer the outline to a sheet of smooth-finish Bristol paper using the method described on page 5.

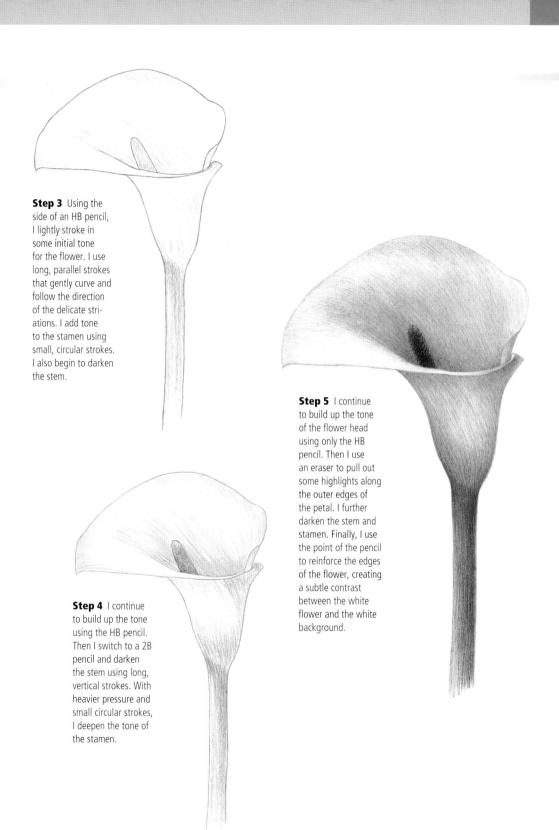

Step 3 Using the side of an HB pencil, I lightly stroke in some initial tone for the flower. I use long, parallel strokes that gently curve and follow the direction of the delicate striations. I add tone to the stamen using small, circular strokes. I also begin to darken the stem.

Step 5 I continue to build up the tone of the flower head using only the HB pencil. Then I use an eraser to pull out some highlights along the outer edges of the petal. I further darken the stem and stamen. Finally, I use the point of the pencil to reinforce the edges of the flower, creating a subtle contrast between the white flower and the white background.

Step 4 I continue to build up the tone using the HB pencil. Then I switch to a 2B pencil and darken the stem using long, vertical strokes. With heavier pressure and small circular strokes, I deepen the tone of the stamen.

TULIP

Tulips come in many varieties and colors, and they are a lot of fun to draw. The stem often curves, so it creates a lovely movement in your drawing. A tulip has a simple cup shape, so if you understand the shading of a cup, it will be much simpler to draw. Try setting up a white teacup under the same lighting conditions to thoroughly understand the shadow patterns.

Combining References Here I combine two different reference photos to create the most pleasing composition. I prefer the flower on the far right to be open, not closed as it is in the photo. So I find another photo of an open tulip and use it to alter the closed tulip in my original reference.

Step 1 Using an HB pencil and tracing vellum, I draw the curves of the stems using long, graceful lines. Then I block in ovals to represent the flower heads. I add irregular ellipses where the insides of the cups are visible. Next I carefully sketch the leaves.

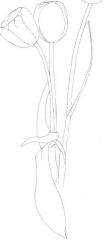

Step 2 Now I draw the petals of the tulips, using the ovals and ellipses as guides. Each tulip is placed at a different angle, so I must be careful to show this. I use mainly curved lines and some oval shapes to draw the petals. Then I study the leaves and refine their shapes as needed.

Step 3 I take a new piece of tracing vellum and place it on top of my drawing. Using my original drawing as a guide, I retrace and refine the flowers, leaves, and stems; then I erase the ellipses, which are no longer necessary. I add some lines to represent a few striations that are seen in the flowers and leaves. When I am satisfied with my drawing, I transfer it to smooth-finish Bristol paper, keeping the lines as light as possible. Then I clean up the drawing with a kneaded eraser.

Step 4 Now it's time to start shading. The light is coming from the left, so I place the shadows and highlights accordingly. Using 2B graphite powder (see page 12), I apply tone to the darkest parts of the tulips with a paper stump. I use curved strokes that follow the form inside the cup and long strokes for the shadowed outer sides of the petals. I apply some graphite to the leaves, then add some tone to the stems near the base of the flower heads.

Step 5 I continue to develop the tone of the tulips with the graphite powder. I add another layer to the open areas of the flowers. I also darken the cast shadow on the middle tulip. Using a larger stump, I further shade the leaves.

Step 6 I use a sharp HB to continue shading the petals and a 2B for the darkest shadows and the insides of the flowers. I switch to a 2H to further define the petal edges. Then I lift out the highlights on the flower heads with a kneaded eraser. For the leaves, I use a 2B pencil and allow the individual strokes to remain visible to create a leaflike texture. I shade the stems like a cylinder, keeping the side facing the light much lighter. Finally, I look at my drawing in a mirror to view it from a fresh perspective so I can see if it needs any final adjustments.

HIBISCUS

This large, brightly colored flower has a distinct shape that makes it a popular choice for tropical designs and patterns. And the way this bloom's impressive size and rippled petals contrast against its long, slender pistil makes it a perfect reference for a portrait study.

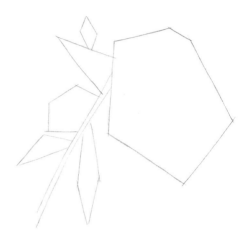

Taking Advantage of Your Surroundings This tropical flower is very popular in gardens in Florida where I live. Look to your surroundings for inspiration and potential drawing subjects!

Step 1 I begin with heavy tracing vellum and use an HB pencil to block in the outer shape of the flower using six straight lines. I also block in the general shapes of the leaves and the closed bud. I check the angle of the stem and the distance between the leaves to be sure I have kept the proper proportions.

Step 2 I start to refine the petals, being mindful of their proportions and angles. At this stage, I still use straight lines to suggest the shapes. I draw a polygon to define the center of the flower, parallel lines for the long filament and style, and polygons to block in the stigma and anther.

Step 3 Now I indicate the major folds of the petals as well as the details of the pistil and stamen. I also draw the details of the bud and sketch light lines to indicate venation on the leaves. At this point, I take another piece of tracing vellum, place it on top of my drawing, and retrace my lines. When I'm pleased with the outline, I transfer the drawing to smooth-finish Bristol paper. Then, with a kneaded eraser, I clean up any unwanted lines.

Step 4 To begin working in tone, I dip a large stump into graphite powder and stroke it into the areas that represent the deepest shadows on the petals and leaves. I apply the deepest tone in the center of the flower.

Step 5 After dipping the stump into graphite powder again, I continue adding lighter tone to the petals. I deepen the cast shadows on the petals and the center of the flower, and I do the same on the leaves. For the thin stems and bud, I use the point of the stump to blend the tone and soften the edges.

Step 6 Now I complete the careful process of shading. I use a sharp HB and stroke over the flower, following the folds of the petals. I deepen the cast shadows with a 2B and darken the center of the flower with a 4B. Next I draw the details of the pistil and stamens, adding some stippling. For the lighter leaf venation, I lift out with a kneaded eraser. I shade the bud delicately, using light pressure. I use the side of a 4B pencil for the branch and make circular strokes to create the rough texture. Then I use a kneaded eraser to clean up any stray lines and finish my drawing.

FREESIA

The freesia has many flower buds on each stem, and the buds open up individually. Each bud and flower must be drawn with precision, but the shapes are based loosely on a cone. Because of the delicacy of the flowers, I use natural, curving shapes to begin my drawing.

Taking Artistic License When taking this photo, I used a dark background so that the white flowers would stand out against the dark values. To reduce clutter in my drawing, I eliminate some of the stems of the flowers and slightly adjust their position.

Step 1 I start my drawing on heavy tracing vellum, using an HB pencil. I study the shapes of the individual flowers and decide to use balloonlike shapes to represent the flowers. I check the proportions and the tilt of the "balloons" to be sure they are placed properly on the stems.

Step 2 I use upside-down U shapes to block in the petals, paying attention to how the petals overlap one another. The smaller flowers at the end are buds, so they do not have defined petals.

Step 3 Now I take a new piece of tracing vellum and use the previous drawing as a guide for my new one. I carefully draw the outline of each petal, refining the shapes. Some of the petals are more angular and pointy, so I make sure to depict that variation. I also add more detail to the sepals at this stage. Then I transfer my work to smooth-finish Bristol paper.

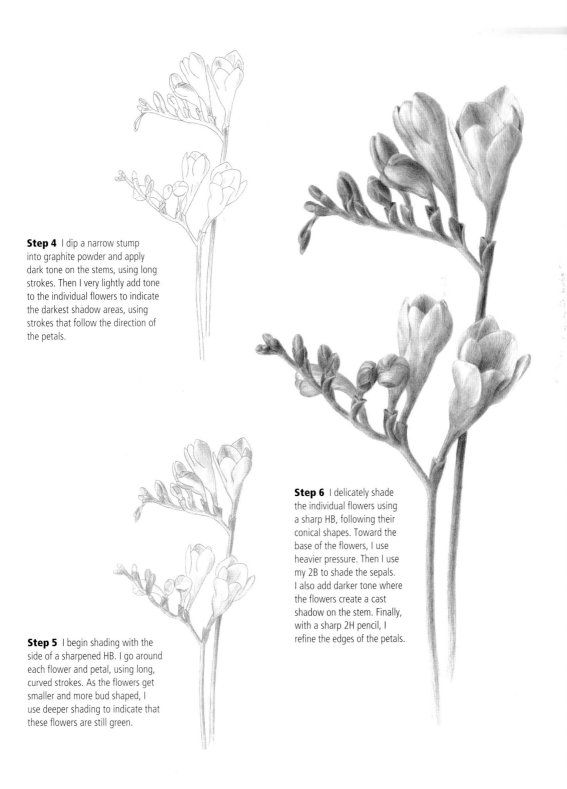

Step 4 I dip a narrow stump into graphite powder and apply dark tone on the stems, using long strokes. Then I very lightly add tone to the individual flowers to indicate the darkest shadow areas, using strokes that follow the direction of the petals.

Step 6 I delicately shade the individual flowers using a sharp HB, following their conical shapes. Toward the base of the flowers, I use heavier pressure. Then I use my 2B to shade the sepals. I also add darker tone where the flowers create a cast shadow on the stem. Finally, with a sharp 2H pencil, I refine the edges of the petals.

Step 5 I begin shading with the side of a sharpened HB. I go around each flower and petal, using long, curved strokes. As the flowers get smaller and more bud shaped, I use deeper shading to indicate that these flowers are still green.

HELICONIA

The heliconia is an exotic tropical plant with colorful, modified leaves called "bracts." Inside each bract is a small flower that sometimes peeks out. Because it is a very flat plant, it can be a challenge to depict it as a three-dimensional object. Therefore, I draw the flower at an angle that shows just a bit of the back side of the bract to give depth to the plant. I add further depth by overlapping the bract and the stem.

Conveying Color Through Value You can depict the bright reds and yellows of this flower with graphite pencil by suggesting different areas of color with different values. To see the values of the colors in your subject, squint your eyes—or simply convert a color image to grayscale using photo-editing software on your computer. In this example, the reds on the bracts have a much darker value than the yellows near the stem.

◀ Step 1 I start with my tracing vellum and an HB pencil and draw the two stems that converge. Then I block in the large shapes of the heliconia flowers, using triangular shapes for the two lower bracts. Next I draw the curved shapes of the bracts within the guidelines. I take another piece of tracing vellum and trace the lines I wish to keep.

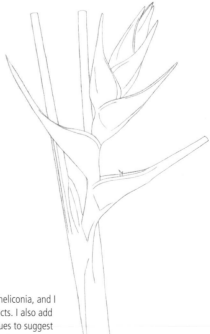

▶ Step 2 I add more details to the stem of the heliconia, and I indicate the border of color changes along the bracts. I also add lines to indicate the area where I'll add darker values to suggest the red color on the bracts. Then I transfer the drawing to a piece of smooth-finish Bristol paper.

◄ Step 3 Now I take a 4B water-soluble graphite pencil and add tone to the stems, stroking along the form. My strokes are close together, forming a fairly even layer of tone. I do not worry about individual lines coming through; I want to add to the textural feeling of the thick stems and dark bracts. To maintain the sense of red color, I use heavier shading. I use long, slightly curved strokes where the form of the bract curves and linear strokes where it straightens out.

▶ Step 4 I dip a watercolor brush in water and gently roll it on a paper towel to absorb excess water and form a point. I start on the stems and drag the brush to allow the water to dissolve the graphite. Wherever I want soft edges, such as along the highlights of the stem, I drag the brush a few more times. I do the same for the bract, using a long, curving stroke. Where the dark red of the bracts meets the yellow of the stem, I soften the edge with extra strokes. At this point, I am just trying to create a softer undertone.

◀ **Step 5** I use the same water-soluble pencil to deepen the tones in the shadowed areas. I use medium pressure along the stems, continuing the long strokes. For the bracts, I again use the heaviest pressure for the deepest values of the flower. To convey the light-valued, yellow areas of the stem near the bracts, I use a very light touch to add just a bit of tone, and where the highlight falls in these areas, I leave the paper white. Then I go over the entire drawing with my watercolor brush, smoothing out the tones.

▶ **Step 6** Now I use a dark 8B water-soluble pencil to further develop the darker tones. I use this along the stem, deepening the shadows. I also darken the deep shadow inside the flower bract. I am careful to capture the striped border along the edge of the flower, using heavy pressure where the bract comes to a point and maintaining the light value of the yellow areas. I again take the watercolor brush and smooth out the tones.

Step 7 When the paper is dry, I take an HB graphite pencil and darken the entire drawing, smoothing out the tones. I use the point of the HB to refine the edges of the flower. Where I need darker tones, I use a 4B pencil. For the darkest darks, I use a sharp point and heavier pressure, particularly along the deep shadows on the stem and along the insides of the bracts. I further smooth out the tones of the flower using both a 2B and an HB. To represent the red color of this tropical plant, I darken the tone with a 2B. Then I use a kneaded eraser to lift out tone, further refining the edges of the bracts and the highlights along the lighter areas of the plant. Instead of applying tone to re-create the value of each color on the bract, I focus on using tone to render the forms. When I'm satisfied with the amount of detail in my drawing, I'm finished!

ORNITHOGALUM

The ornithogalum is an unusual flower in that it grows on several stalks that extend from the main stem, so each stem holds many flowers. The ornithogalum features bracts, much like the heliconia, but here the flowers extend past the bracts and are visible. Although it may look very complex, the flower becomes much more approachable when you think of the flowers as being shaped like wide cups.

Finding Inspiration
I spotted this flower in a local nursery and couldn't resist taking it home for a "photo shoot." This particular plant has an elegant curve to the stem, which leads the eye up to the naturally formed "bouquet" of flowers.

Step 1 Starting on my tracing vellum, I use an HB pencil to draw the stem and leaves, carefully mimicking the way the stalk bends and forks. The leaves have a triangular shape that ends in a curve. I block in cup shapes to represent the flowers, flattening some and making others more pointed.

Step 2 Now I draw the individual petal shapes within the guidelines, using curved lines that come to a point. Think of each flower as a cup viewed from a slightly different angle. When the view is from above, the stamens and pistils are visible.

Step 3 I transfer my art to a new sheet of tracing vellum. I erase the guidelines and refine the petals, indicating subtle variations in their curves. I add a few curved lines to show the midline of some of the petals, which also helps give direction to the form. I do the same for the upper cluster. Then I move my work to a sheet of smooth-finish Bristol paper.

Step 4 I use graphite powder to apply dark tones on the stem, leaves, and upper part of the stalk. I also add some tone to the shadows on the upper cluster and the visible stigma, as well as to the insides of the leaves.

Step 6 I use a sharp HB to delicately shade the flower petals. I lift out areas that are directly in the light. Then I use a sharp 2B to darken areas of the flowers that are turned away from the light, and I draw the small cast shadows created by the petals. Still using the 2B, I draw the pistil and then use a 4B to add stippling to the anther for texture. Next I switch back to the 2B pencil to shade the upper part of the stalk with curved strokes. I also shade the stem and leaves, using long parallel strokes; then I switch to a 4B for the areas that turn away from the light. I use heavy pressure with the 4B to create the deep tones inside the leaves and for the cast shadows under the flowers. I go over the edges with my HB pencil to delineate the petals.

Step 5 I add another layer of graphite powder for the deepest shadows. Then I add very light tone to the flowers, paying careful attention to where the light hits. I make my strokes follow the form of each object.

WATER LILY

This lovely lily was floating in a small pond near my home. I use mostly horizontal strokes instead of curves for this pretty aquatic plant. The horizontal strokes show the flatness of the huge leaves as they float on the surface of the water.

Revisiting Your Artist's Morgue It's always a good idea to periodically scan your photo collection, often called an "artist's morgue." Storing your references digitally allows you to categorize and review your collection easily. I had taken this photo so many years ago that I nearly had forgotten all about it!

Step 1 I study my reference to look for the basic shapes; then, using an HB pencil on heavy tracing vellum, I block in the large oval shapes for the lily pads. I see the flower as a rounded triangular form, with two long oval shapes at the base.

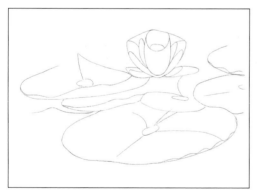

Step 2 Using the initial guidelines, I draw the basic shapes of the flower petals. Then I use ovals to delineate the centers of the lily pads where some water collects. I use long wavy lines to indicate folds in the lily pads and then indicate some of the major veins.

Step 3 Now I transfer the art to a new piece of tracing vellum, excluding the guidelines. I carefully render the flower and the stamens peeking out in the center. I also add the major venation lines of the lily pads and draw in some small circles to indicate the highlights. Then I use a few horizontal strokes to begin the water. Now I move my drawing to a piece of smooth-finish Bristol paper.

Step 4 I use a stump and graphite powder to lay down tone across the water and lily pads, always using horizontal strokes. I add a few additional strokes along the venation lines. Using the point of the stump, I lightly shade the flower petals, following their form. I then switch to a 2B pencil and continue to deepen the tones on the water and lily pads, using mostly horizontal strokes.

Step 5 I continue to refine and deepen the tones, now using only the pencil and horizontal strokes. I work mostly with the 2B and the 4B, using the HB pencil only for edge details. I shade the flower with an HB and a 2B, again using strokes that follow the form of the petals. I am careful to add the dark shadows where the pads lift up a bit and where they fold. To finish, I lift out the highlights using the tip of a kneaded eraser.

CLEMATIS

The clematis is a lovely star-shaped flower that can climb and twist around fences like a vine. Because it often is entwined with another object, it can become quite complex to draw. In order to simplify my job, I choose to depict only one flower, creating a pleasing design with the main leaves and stems that surround it.

Being Prepared Carry a camera with you as often as possible, because you never know where inspiration will strike! For example, I snapped this clematis reference outside a shop while running errands.

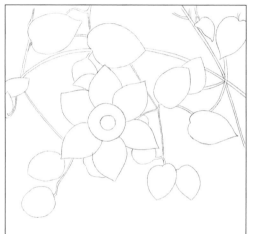

◄ **Step 1** On a piece of tracing vellum, I draw the star shape of the flower with an HB pencil, taking note of which petals overlap. I use circles to represent the central pistils and stamens to simplify the composition.

► **Step 2** Now I add the lines of the supporting lattice. Because I want to create a realistic representation of this pretty vine, I use a ruler to draw straight, parallel lines.

◄ **Step 3** Here I move my work to a new piece of tracing vellum and add the little curves along the edges of the petals. Using the circles as my guide, I draw lines to represent the stigma and pistils. Next I look for the main veins of the leaves and draw them, and then I add details to the bud on the left.

Step 4 After transferring the drawing to smooth-finish Bristol paper, I add tone to the leaves with graphite powder and a stump but leave the flower white for now. Then I rub graphite onto the lattice, allowing some of my strokes to go outside the lines to indicate the cast shadows on the wall.

Step 5 I add darker tone to the leaves to show the shadowed areas. I also make very light, radial strokes along the middle of each flower petal; then I add some short, darker strokes closer to the center of the flower. Using the point of the stump, I darken the recessed areas of the lattice.

Step 6 I continue to darken the leaves and the lattice. I use a 2B pencil to even out the tones and refine the shading; then I switch between the pencil and the stump for a more painterly look. For the darkest parts of the lattice, I use a 4B pencil. I finish shading the flower petals with a sharp HB, leaving the edges white so they contrast with the dark background. Then I darken the very center of the flower with a 2B, carefully drawing the pistils and stamens. Finally, I clean up the drawing using my kneaded eraser.

CREATING TEXTURE

Hydrangeas are a sturdy perennial shrub found in many gardens. Their large flowers actually are made of many little florets. Rather than draw each tiny floret, I want to create the illusion that there are many small blossoms. To do so, I use vellum-finish Bristol paper, which has a slight texture; the fine tooth of this paper provides a grainy quality to pencil strokes that can enhance the surfaces of many subjects. In this case, the paper boosts the textures of the flowers and the pot.

Finding a Good Composition This pretty pot bursting with flowers was sitting on top of a wall covered with vine. The perfect still-life setup was there waiting for me—all I had to do was draw!

Step 1 I begin this drawing on heavy tracing vellum. Picking up an HB pencil, I start with the vase, using a simple outline. I represent the hydrangea with an irregular circular shape. Then I block in bubble shapes to indicate where the flowers will be. Next I add a few heart shapes to represent the leaves.

Step 2 I transfer my drawing to a new piece of tracing vellum. Now I create the woven texture of the pot, using small ellipses and lines that curve around the pot. I add more irregular flower shapes and draw the most prominent leaves. I place some leaves and branches for the ivy. Then I move the drawing to vellum-finish Bristol paper.

Step 3 With a 6B pencil, I lightly shade the flowers. Then I darken the shadowed side of the vase. Using the point of the pencil, I add tone to the darkest areas of the leaves. I switch to my stump and graphite powder to smudge the darker leaves. Where the light hits the leaves, I use a lighter touch. I use the same method to smudge the ivy, and I add more tone with a 2B.

Step 4 Using the 6B, I focus on refining the outline of each individual flower. I use my kneaded eraser to pick out the light areas of the flowers. Then I trace over the outlines of the leaves using a sharp HB. Alternating between a 2B pencil and the point of a narrow stump, I add darker tone to the leaves. I pick out a few light areas with my eraser and then follow the same process to shade the ivy. I add form shading to the vase with a 6B and then draw short, curved strokes with a 2B to create the texture.

Step 5 I use a dull 6B pencil to stipple additional texture on the flowers. I refine the leaves, adding more detail and tone with a sharp 2B. With a very sharp HB, I reinforce the vertical lines of the weave of the vase. I allow some of the texture to be lost in the shadows. For the ivy, I use a 4B in the deepest shadow areas. I add the details of the leaves with a sharp HB pencil, and then I use a 2B to draw in the branches. To complete my drawing, I add some light diagonal lines along the side of the pot to create the background, adding more depth to the image.

COMPOSING A SCENE

A box of flowers on a windowsill is a common sight in many neighborhoods. This one just happens to make a nice composition! I make a few adjustments to my reference, however: I scoot the geraniums toward the center of the window, so the window acts as a frame. I also want the focal point to be the geraniums, not the window, so I keep the flowers lighter in value than the background for a contrast that makes them really "pop." To emphasize the rough texture of the stone, which nicely contrasts with the smooth glass of the window, I combine charcoal with a rougher, vellum-finish Bristol paper.

Making Changes I remind myself often that I'm not a slave to my photo reference. I wanted a prettier pot for this scene, so when I found one, I worked it into the drawing.

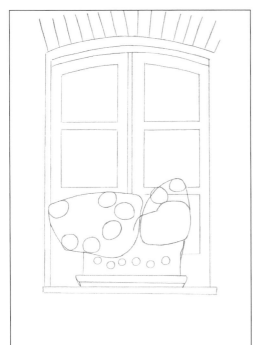

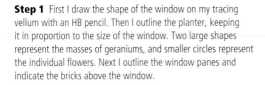

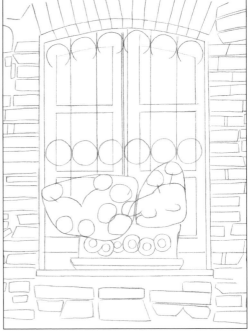

Step 1 First I draw the shape of the window on my tracing vellum with an HB pencil. Then I outline the planter, keeping it in proportion to the size of the window. Two large shapes represent the masses of geraniums, and smaller circles represent the individual flowers. Next I outline the window panes and indicate the bricks above the window.

Step 2 I draw in the circles of the wrought iron and place the lines of the bars using a ruler. Then I pencil in the bricks. A few curved lines among the flower masses represent the major leaves. I also draw double circles on the planter to block in its floral design.

Step 3 Now I transfer my work to another piece of tracing vellum, excluding the guidelines. I add more details, starting with the wrought iron. Then I move to the bricks, putting in a more irregular outline that is characteristic of old buildings. Next I draw the flowers, keeping them somewhat uneven. I draw in the petals of the flower detail on the planter last. Now I can transfer my work to a sheet of vellum-finish Bristol paper.

Step 4 I lightly go over my outlines with a sharp B carbon pencil. Then I go over the bricks with the side of a stick of vine charcoal. Vine charcoal is very soft and can be erased easily. With a stump and some charcoal powder, I use long strokes to place the dark tone of the wood frame. I smudge in some tone for the leaves; then I add tone to the planter with a very light touch.

Step 5 Using my stump, I smear charcoal on the bricks. Then I apply another light layer of charcoal over both the bricks and the grout, creating a rough texture. I add another layer of charcoal on the windowpanes and then smear it with the stump, keeping the tops of the windowpanes very light. I darken the tones in the leaf areas; then I add just a touch of charcoal to the flowers, but I do not smear it.

Step 6 With the same sharp B carbon pencil, I refine and re-outline the more prominent leaves. Then I add some additional tone with the pencil to further define the shadows on the leaves. Next I use the point of the pencil to give some texture to the flowers using very short, curved strokes. I deepen the tone of the wood of the window by adding carbon pencil and smearing the strokes.

Step 7 Using the side of the carbon pencil with a light touch, I add more tone to the brick in an irregular manner to create the variations in texture. I lightly dab the tone with an eraser to create lighter areas for even more variation. I draw some uneven lines at the bottoms of the bricks to create a sense of depth, and I darken the wood with the carbon pencil, using strokes that follow the wood grain. With a very sharp point, I re-outline the edges of the wood and also the wrought iron. I add further detail to the leaves, using very heavy pressure in the deep shadow areas. Then I add more detail to the flowers with short strokes. Using the stump, I add a very light tone to the middle window panes, and I add some diagonal strokes along the top. I deepen the tone of the lowest window panes by using some more carbon pencil and smearing the tone with the stump. Then I very carefully shade the planter, leaving the floral decoration lighter. Finally, I use the sharp B carbon pencil to add the details of the embroidery on the curtain.

SIMPLIFYING A DRAWING

Looking at a field of sunflowers is like looking at field of happy faces. When choosing a viewpoint for this cheerful flower, I decide on a straight-on view to better capture the flower's personality. Because I want to focus on the unique features of this flower and showcase its character, I simplify the composition and draw just one flower, adding a nondescript scene in the distance for the background.

Using Multiple References I use a composite of three photos for this drawing: one for the flower head, another for the stalk, and another for a background that won't draw attention away from the focal point—the single sunflower.

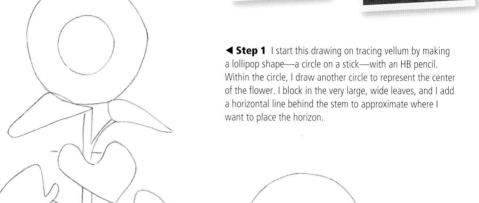

◄ Step 1 I start this drawing on tracing vellum by making a lollipop shape—a circle on a stick—with an HB pencil. Within the circle, I draw another circle to represent the center of the flower. I block in the very large, wide leaves, and I add a horizontal line behind the stem to approximate where I want to place the horizon.

► Step 2 I extend the horizon line, making it curvy to represent hills. Then I add a few outlines for the trees in the distance. Next I place few more details, such as the center veins on the leaves.

40

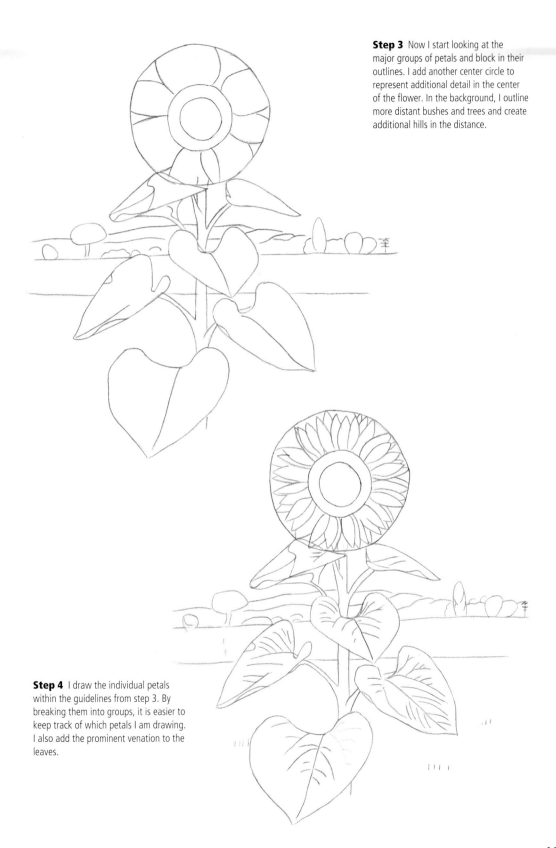

Step 3 Now I start looking at the major groups of petals and block in their outlines. I add another center circle to represent additional detail in the center of the flower. In the background, I outline more distant bushes and trees and create additional hills in the distance.

Step 4 I draw the individual petals within the guidelines from step 3. By breaking them into groups, it is easier to keep track of which petals I am drawing. I also add the prominent venation to the leaves.

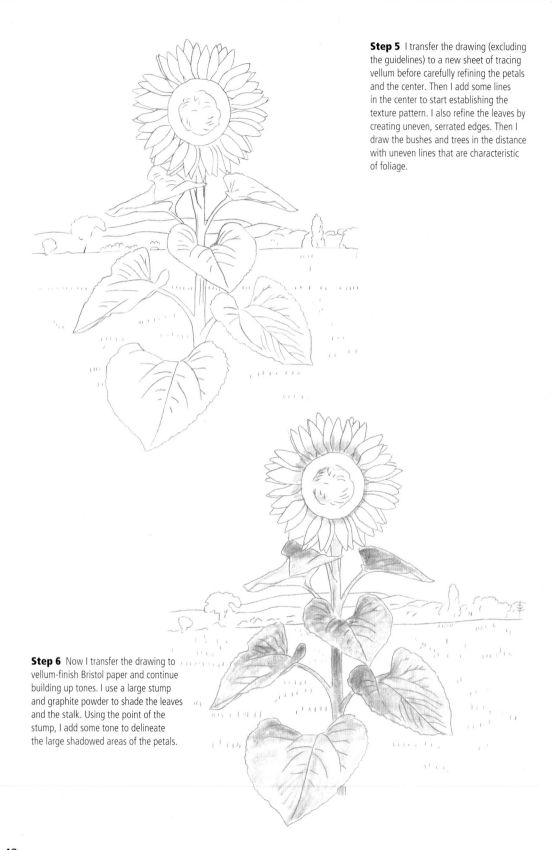

Step 5 I transfer the drawing (excluding the guidelines) to a new sheet of tracing vellum before carefully refining the petals and the center. Then I add some lines in the center to start establishing the texture pattern. I also refine the leaves by creating uneven, serrated edges. Then I draw the bushes and trees in the distance with uneven lines that are characteristic of foliage.

Step 6 Now I transfer the drawing to vellum-finish Bristol paper and continue building up tones. I use a large stump and graphite powder to shade the leaves and the stalk. Using the point of the stump, I add some tone to delineate the large shadowed areas of the petals.

Step 7 Using the side of a 6B pencil and light pressure, I add tone to the center of the flower. Then I add a bit more shading to the darker parts of the petals. I use a 2B pencil to make curved lines that follow the direction of the petals. With my stump, I add more graphite to the leaves and stems. I accentuate the shadowed parts of the leaves by adding even more graphite.

Step 8 Going back to my 6B pencil, I deepen the tones in the center of the flower. I add more shading to the individual petals, particularly to the petals in the back, using a 2B. For the leaves, I further model the shapes using a stump and graphite powder. Then I lift out the veins in the leaves. I also add tone to the background with a stump and graphite powder, using circular strokes for the bushes and trees. Next I smudge in some texture for the cornfield in the distance using vertical strokes.

Step 9 I go back and refine the petals with the 2B pencil and the center of the flower with the side of the 6B. I add more tone to the leaves and stems with a 2B, then smear them with a stump. I use my kneaded eraser to again lift out any veins that begin to get lost. I work on the landscape, first with the stump and graphite powder and then with the side of a 4B to add some texture to the bushes and trees. I also add vertical lines to the cornfield using the side of a 2B.

Portraying Distance

Atmospheric perspective dictates that as objects recede into the distance, they become less and less detailed. The illustration here is a good example of this concept. For the foreground flower, I draw every petal with extreme detail. On the middle-ground flower, I roughly draw the petals, but not every single one. For the three distant flowers, I pencil circular shapes, darkening only the centers. The most distant flowers are just stippled dots.

Step 10 Now I refine the drawing by using a sharp 2B to continue modeling the petals. I do the same for the leaves and stems, but I alternate between smudging and using the pencil to achieve a somewhat smoother texture. I accentuate the shadows and use the kneaded eraser to lift out the highlights of the leaves. Then I make short lines to create the small shadow cast underneath the flower's center. I further refine the texture of the center using the side of a 4B. Next I define the distant bushes and trees, still using the 4B, and I add a few branches to the tree on the left. I continue to build up the cornfield texture using both vertical lines and short, curved lines. For the texture of the middle- and foreground, I lightly smudge some tone and then draw short vertical lines. Lastly, I check for any final adjustments and clean up my drawing with a kneaded eraser.

INCORPORATING INK WASHES

For this project, I want to achieve a soft, dark appearance, so I decide to incorporate an ink wash. The ink wash works like watercolor paint, creating a loose, blended look. I also decide to use vellum-finish Bristol paper to include some built-in texture.

Taking Advantage of Landscaping Stylish landscaping is a wonderful source of inspiration for botanical drawings. Often the plants and flowers already are arranged in a pleasing manner, with contrasting textures and values waiting for you to replicate them!

Step 1 After studying my photo reference, I break down the scene into a few basic shapes on a piece of tracing vellum. With an HB pencil, I block in the groups of flowers and foliage with two large oval shapes. Then I add the tall shapes of the columns. I draw a horizontal line under the trees for the ground and add the general outlines of the two main trees.

Step 2 I add detail to the columns and break up the foliage by adding smaller ovals to indicate the main groups of leaves and flowers. I create the border around the plants and add a few lines to map out the main shapes of the middle ground. I also add the upper outline of trees in the distance.

Step 3 After adding details on the iron work and columns, I further delineate the foliage and flower masses. I use lines to indicate the direction of the foliage masses in the middle- and background. Then I add the stone detail of the border.

Step 4 I place another piece of tracing vellum on top of my drawing and trace the scene, leaving out the original guidelines. Then I add some more flowers in the foreground. When I'm happy with the drawing, I transfer it to vellum-finish Bristol paper.

Step 5 Now I apply an extremely light ink wash over the background area. (See "Mixing Ink Washes" on page 49.) I dilute some India ink with water and apply a thin layer of the mixture over the deeper shadowed areas of foliage. After washing some tone over the two prominent trees in the background, I apply a light wash on the path.

Step 6 I apply a very light wash to the columns. Then I mix a slightly darker wash (more ink and less water) and apply it to the shadowed areas of the foliage, as well as to the background. I also add some tone over the border stone. I switch to a small brush and use a fairly dark wash to "draw" the ironwork. When the ink and paper are dry, I use a 6B pencil to shade the trees in the background.

Step 7 I add another dark wash to the darkest areas; when the wash is dry, I finish the shading with pencils. I use the side of a 4B to lightly add some broken tone to the background. I shade the columns using the side of a 2B, switching to an HB for the columns' details. I use a 4B and a 6B to apply additional deep tone to the left side of the drawing and the foliage on the right, just behind the path. With the point of a 2B, I draw some vertical lines to indicate tree trunks in the background. Then I add texture to the two main trees with a 4B. I draw the ironwork with a 2B pencil. For the flowers, I alternate between a 2B and a 4B pencil, and then I lift out tone with a kneaded eraser. I use the point of a 2B to draw more of the stone detail, switching to the side of a 2B to add uneven tone to the stones.

Mixing Ink Washes

Occasionally I use India ink to add dynamism to my drawings. It can be used on its own to create a very black tone or diluted with distilled water to create different values. Adjusting the amount of water you use in your ink washes provides a range of values. When creating a wash, it is best to start with the lightest value and build up to a darker value, rather than adding water to a dark wash to lighten it. To learn how to mix various values, create a value chart like the one shown below. Start with a very diluted wash, and gradually add more ink for successively darker values.

RENDERING ROSES

There is probably no flower that expresses romance like a rose. To faithfully capture this elegant flower, you must remember two important things: First, you must carefully place the light source so the individual petals are visible—without proper lighting, the petals will become an indistinguishable mass. Second, draw each petal with care and precision so that the angle of each petal is accurate and the blossom opens correctly.

Taking Multiple Photos Even though this is not a very complex arrangement, I spend a lot of time taking photos of different angles of the flower. I also play with the values of the background elements until the subject "pops" to my liking.

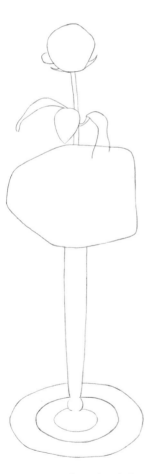

Step 1 Starting on tracing vellum, I draw the basic shapes of the vase with an HB pencil. Then I compare the shape and size of the baby's breath with the vase and block in the general mass. Next I add the stem of the rose, the leaves, and the flower. Ellipses represent the lace at the bottom of the vase.

Step 2 I draw the rose petals within the guidelines. Next I block in the main groups of the tiny baby's breath. I add the stem and water line to the bud vase, and then I add more detail to the crocheted lace.

Types of Vases

Here are some drawings of vases that I have collected in my studio. Keep an eye out for the many different shapes of vases. By changing the size and shape of the vase, your composition changes. For example, a long, thin vase brings a dramatic sense of space to your drawing; and a short, wide bowl draws the viewer's eye horizontally across the composition. Experiment with different vases and see what works!

Step 3 After I add further detail to the leaves, I draw some of the main veins. I also add more lines in the vase to indicate the stems and leaves. I make little circles to define the delicate flowers, and I add a bit more detail to the lace.

Step 4 Now I place another piece of tracing vellum on top of the drawing to clean up the outline. I refine the petals, also adding more blossoms in the baby's breath. Then I add detail to the lace.

◄ Step 5 Now I transfer my art to a sheet of smooth-finish Bristol paper. Then, using a small stump and graphite powder, I lightly lay in some tone on the darkest shadow areas—this includes the leaves, the stem, and the cast shadow on the table.

► Step 6 With the point of a very small stump and some graphite powder, I delicately add tone to the petals. I start with the areas in deepest shadow, building up tone to create form and dimension. Using long strokes, I darken the long stem. I add more tone to the leaves and then lightly touch tone onto the lace to represent the cast shadow.

◄ Step 7 I use an HB pencil to lightly shade the rose, following the form of the petals. I do the same for the leaves, deepening the shadowed areas with a 2B. I very lightly apply the side of the 2B to the baby's breath so that the paper picks up just a bit of speckled tone. Then I use the 2B and long strokes to deepen the stem and the vase. I also add very light detailing to the lace.

► Step 8 I go back and refine the shading of the rose petals with an HB, using a very delicate touch. I deepen the leaves with a 2B and return to the HB for drawing the edge detail and the areas that are in the strongest light. For the baby's breath, I alternate between adding some light tone with the side of a 2B and lifting out tone with a kneaded eraser. For the reflections in the vase, I lift out tone in the light areas and deepen some of the darker tones with an HB. I use very heavy pressure with a 2B for the stem shadows, and I stipple in the holes of the lace, lightly adding more tone on top. After I deepen the cast shadow on the table, my drawing is complete!

APPROACHING ARRANGEMENTS

When creating an arrangement of mixed flowers, I like to use a variety of shapes to build an interesting composition. By combining long, thin plants with leaves, flowers, and buds, my composition gains variation in height, depth, value, and texture. Don't be afraid to work with several different elements; everything can be broken down into simple shapes.

Keeping It Simple When setting up a floral still life, keep the ground, background, and even the vase simple, using textural qualities that won't overwhelm the flowers.

◀ **Step 1** Using my photo reference, I analyze this rather complex arrangement by looking for the largest basic shapes created by the flowers and leaves. On a piece of tracing vellum, I use an HB pencil to draw a simple cup shape for the copper pot and a large oval for the mass of foliage and flowers. I make sure the proportion of this shape is correct in relation to the size of the pot. Then I draw smaller shapes for the larger masses of leaves and flowers.

▶ **Step 2** Now I start to block in the main details, beginning with the basic shapes of the flowers. Then I draw the most prominent leaves. I also add long cigar shapes to represent the lavender stalks. I add the handle and a few more details to the pot and establish the angle of the cast shadow.

Step 3 I take a new piece of heavy tracing vellum and place it on top of the initial drawing. Using the previously drawn areas as a guide, I create a very detailed drawing of the flower arrangement. I draw the shapes of the lavender, add detail to the buds, and carefully refine the petals. Then I add more detail to the leaves and draw some of the smaller leaves. I also draw a few more lines to indicate the details of the pot.

Step 4 I transfer my drawing to a sheet of smooth-finish Bristol paper and erase any unwanted lines, and then I look at the arrangement while squinting. This blurs the details and helps me see the variations in value. Using a large stump and graphite powder, I place some tone where I see the deepest values, mostly at the base of the foliage.

Step 5 I return with the stump and graphite powder and begin to establish a darker tone for most of the leaves, except where they are in the strongest light. I darken the shadowed foliage, and then I use a smaller stump to apply some tonal variation to the buds and the flowers. For the lavender stalk, I use a 6B pencil and make small, irregular, circular strokes. Using the large stump again, I begin to add tone to the shadowed side of the pot.

Step 6 Now I use a 2B pencil to deepen and refine the tones. I start with the darker leaves, using strokes that follow their forms. With tiny circular strokes, I add tone to the stamens. Then I shade the buds and the lighter flowers with an HB pencil and a very light touch. Using the side of a 2B and very short, quick strokes, I create a rough texture for the lavender stalks. For the pot, I use long, curved strokes, paying attention to the distinct reflections of the metal. Where the light hits the pot, I leave the paper white. (See "Reflective Surfaces" on page 57.)

Step 7 I continue refining the drawing, alternating between an HB for lighter tones and a 2B for darker tones. For the darkest areas, I work with both a 4B and a 2B. I also refine the pot, working with an HB for sharp details and a 2B for darker tones. With an HB pencil, I stipple the spots of the lily. For the leaves, I alternate between shading with a 2B and lifting out tone with a kneaded eraser to create the venation. I lightly shade the cloth with the side of a 6B, allowing the grain of the paper to break up the strokes. When I am satisfied, I erase any stray marks.

Reflective Surfaces

To capture the realistic surface of a vase, it is important to study how the vase reflects light. The highlights on an object help give it form and depth and define its shape. On shiny objects, such as glass or polished metal, highlights are very distinct with sharp edges. On dull materials, such as wood or unglazed ceramics, the highlights are not well-defined. Try setting up a metal object under a strong light and look for the highlights. Replicate the highlights in your drawing, either by leaving that area of the paper white or lifting out tone with an eraser. Here the first vase is slick and has a sharp, defined highlight, whereas the second vase is dull and the highlight is very blurry.

DRAWING WHAT YOU LOVE

Everyone has a wealth of experiences to draw from. My dear neighbor grew up in Japan and recently gave me a cherished gift from her homeland. This simple little teacup represents an important part of her culture—the tea ceremony—and it adds a personal touch to this contemporary floral arrangement.

When drawing this scene, I use the negative space of the elements of the floral arrangement to create an engaging composition. The negative space often is as important as the focal elements, providing balance and unity. Negative space also offers contrast in line, values, texture, and shapes to heighten interest in the composition.

Arranging a Composition I set up this arrangement so that the focal point (the flower arrangement) is slightly off center; it is balanced by the long, looping leaves on the left, which create an interesting series of negative shapes.

Step 1 First I break down this fairly complex setup into basic shapes on a piece of tracing vellum. Using my reference photo, I study the objects and look for large shapes that help simplify the arrangement. I use a large oval shape to describe the vase and the mass of leaves. I also draw two ovals to block in the flowers that protrude from the main mass. With an HB pencil, I carefully draw the curved lines to represent the long, thin leaves on the left. I use a flattened oval for the tea cup and an elliptical shape for the saucer.

Step 2 I double-check that the proportions of the basic shapes are correct, and then I add ovals to represent the centers of the flowers. I draw the shapes of the protruding leaves on the left of the main mass. Next I indicate the inside of the cup with an ellipse. Then I add two leaves that extend from the main mass on the lower right side. I also add the shapes of the most evident leaves, and I draw a curved line on the lower right to show the outline of the bottom right of the vase.

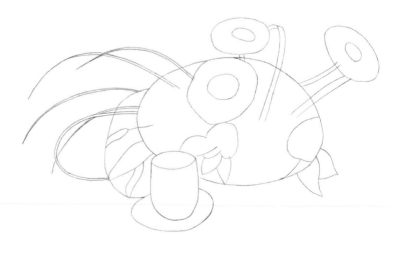

Step 3 Now I focus on breaking down the petal shapes. I look for the groupings of petals rather than drawing each individual petal. I define the very center of the flower with another oval. Then I add some more leaves to the main leaf mass and further define the leaves that were drawn in step 2.

Step 4 Using another piece of tracing vellum, I redraw the main shapes and details, eliminating the initial basic shapes. As I do this, I refine the leaves on the lower right and add another protruding leaf on the left.

Step 5 I add the berries and more individual leaves. The advantage of using overlays of tracing vellum is particularly evident in a complex drawing such as this; I can continue to overlay and correct as many times as I like until I am satisfied with the drawing.

Step 6 Now I draw the petals of the flowers. I also add more details to the leaves and berries and further define the ferns. The saucer has a rather odd shape, so I refine the lines a bit. I transfer the drawing to smooth-finish Bristol paper and then make any necessary corrections with a sharp HB pencil. Next I clean up the drawing with a kneaded eraser.

Step 7 Using a 4B water-soluble pencil, I apply tone on the long leaves. I draw long lines for the outer petals, using heavier pressure for shadows; I use short, curved strokes for the petals in the center. I shade with the side of the pencil for the leaves, using heavy pressure for dark shadows. I switch to carbon dust to add tone to the teacup and dish, blending both with a stump.

Step 8 I run a damp, small round watercolor brush along the length of the thin leaves. Then I use short strokes on the flowers to blend the graphite, dragging some tone into the lighter areas and leaving only the highlights white. In the center of the flower and on the berries, I use circular strokes. With an HB pencil, I lightly draw the birds on the teacup. Then I use a bit more carbon dust to add tone to the cup.

CLOSING THOUGHTS

It is my hope that the end of this book marks the beginning of your journey toward capturing the beauty of flowers and botanicals. With careful study, even the most complex flowers or flower arrangements can be broken down into basic shapes. By using these shapes as a guide for building tone and creating texture and depth, you soon will be growing a garden of beautiful drawings in your studio!